THE LAST SUPPER

LEADER GUIDE

The Last Supper
Conversations That Led to the Cross

The Last Supper

978-1-7910-3738-3

978-1-7910-3739-0 eBook

The Last Supper: DVD

978-1-7910-3742-0

The Last Supper: Leader Guide

978-1-7910-3740-6

978-1-7910-3741-3 eBook

Also by Will Willimon

The Church We Carry:
Loss, Leadership, and the Future of the Church

Changing My Mind:
The Overlooked Virtue for Faithful Ministry

Heaven and Earth:
Advent and the Incarnation

THE LAST SUPPER

Conversations That Led to the Cross

WILL WILLIMON

Abingdon Press | Nashville

The Last Supper
Conversations That Led to the Cross
Leader Guide

Copyright © 2025 Abingdon Press
All rights reserved.

978-1-7910-3740-6

Scripture quotations are taken from the Common English Bible, copyright 2011. Used by permission. All rights reserved.

Book cover description for *The Last Supper: Conversations That Led to the Cross Leader Guide* by Will Willimon. The top half shows the title in large white capital letters, with "THE" above a black line and "LAST SUPPER" stacked below. The background features a colorful, abstract illustration of Jesus and several disciples at the table, rendered with overlapping geometric shapes in vibrant shades of blue, red, orange, green, and yellow. At the top, a black banner with white text reads: "LEADER GUIDE." Below the artwork, a beige strip holds the subtitle in black serif text. The author's name appears at the bottom in large white serif letters on a dark, multicolored background.

CONTENTS

View a complimentary session
of Will Willimon's
The Last Supper

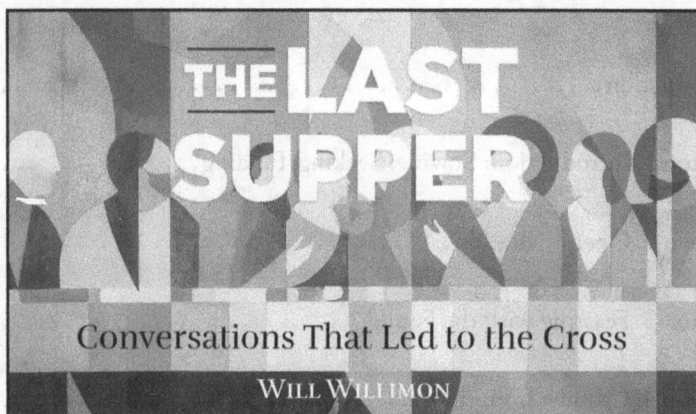

Scan the QR code below or visit
https://bit.ly/thelastsupper
_session1.

Introduction

In *The Last Supper: Conversations That Led to the Cross*, Will Willimon invites readers to follow Jesus on his final journey from Palm Sunday to Easter, listening carefully to the parables he tells along the way. But be warned: Willimon calls these stories "riddles" rather than simple moral lessons, and he insists they're primarily about God's character rather than our behavior. As he puts it with characteristic bluntness, "Want to get close to Jesus? You'll have to sit for story time with him."

This Leader Guide has been written to help you lead a group of adults through Willimon's challenging and transformative study. Each of its six session plans corresponds to a chapter in *The Last Supper*:

+ **Session 1: Introduction; Sowing, Seeking, Finding**—Jesus
begins his final week not with a military campaign but with
stories about God's reckless grace. Participants will explore the
parable of the Sower and the good Samaritan, discovering that
God's kingdom operates by different mathematics than our
world's kingdoms.

+ **Session 2: Open Invitation**—Jesus crashes dinner parties with
radical instructions about hospitality and inclusion. Participants
will wrestle with the Great Banquet parable and confront their
own "good excuses" for avoiding God's expansive invitation to
unlikely guests.

+ **Session 3: Feasting with the Found**—Through the beloved
stories of lost sheep, lost coins, and the prodigal son, participants
will recognize themselves as both lost and found, both grateful
recipients and grumbling older brothers. They'll discover that
these are stories about God's scandalous grace rather than
human morality.

+ **Session 4: Crumbs from the Table**—Perhaps the most
challenging session, participants will confront Jesus's
uncomfortable teachings about wealth and poverty through
the parable of Lazarus and the rich man, balanced with the
hopeful example of Zacchaeus. Expect resistance; Willimon
admits his own defensiveness about these texts.

+ **Session 5: Refusing the Host**—As Jesus approaches Jerusalem,
his parables grow darker, revealing our tendency to treat God's
gifts as our possessions and reject God's authority. Participants
will explore the violence inherent in refusing God's messengers
while finding hope in God's persistent love.

+ **Session 6: The Host Becomes the Meal**—The journey
culminates in the Last Supper, where Jesus embodies all his
parables in bread and wine. Participants will connect Maundy
Thursday to Emmaus and discover that every communion
continues Jesus's radical table fellowship.

Although this Leader Guide assumes all participants are reading *The
Last Supper*, its extensive quotations from Willimon's book and inclusion of
key scripture passages mean leaders can also use it effectively on its own.
The study is designed for flexibility—whether your group meets in person,
virtually, or in a hybrid format.

Each session contains the following elements to draw from as you plan
six weekly gatherings:

+ **Session Goals**—reflecting Willimon's theological priorities
+ **Biblical Foundations**—Key scripture passages for each session

+ **Before Your Session**—Preparation tips, including warnings about potential resistance to challenging material
+ **Starting Your Session**—Discussion questions to help participants engage with the material
+ **Opening Prayer**—Written in Willimon's conversational, accessible style
+ **Main Discussion Sections**—Built around Willimon's key insights and interpretations
+ **Closing Your Session**—A practical activity plus Willimon's own discussion questions from each chapter
+ **Closing Prayer**—Reflecting the session's themes and theological challenges

A Word About Willimon's Approach

Will Willimon doesn't offer easy comfort or simple moral lessons. He insists that Jesus's parables are "riddles" that reveal God's kingdom to be radically different from our expectations. As he warns early in the book, "God's realm is so different from our kingdoms that when Jesus is revealing, sometimes it feels like he's concealing."

This means participants may often feel more puzzled than comforted by these sessions. That's intentional. Willimon believes that "better than understanding Jesus is to be at table with Jesus." The goal isn't to solve Jesus's riddles but to be transformed by encountering the God they reveal.

Expect resistance, especially in Sessions 2, 4, and 5, which deal with economic justice, radical inclusion, and accountability. Willimon models honesty about his own defensiveness, and leaders should be prepared to acknowledge their own discomfort while maintaining Jesus's challenging message.

Theological Themes to Emphasize

Throughout your leadership, keep these key Willimonesque insights in mind:

- **Parables Are About God, Not Us:** Resist the temptation to turn every parable into a moral lesson. Focus first on what the story reveals about God's character, then consider implications for discipleship.

- **God's Initiative, Not Ours:** From the reckless sower to the seeking shepherd to the pursuing father, these stories emphasize God's relentless pursuit of us rather than our search for God.

- **Scandalous Grace:** God's love operates by different mathematics than worldly fairness. The kingdom celebrates wasteful generosity over prudent management.

- **Radical Hospitality:** Jesus's table fellowship with sinners culminates in a Last Supper where betrayers are welcomed. The church continues this scandalous hospitality.

- **Active Hope:** Willimon insists that active hope applies to all of Jesus's kingdom parables. They call us to join God's work, not wait passively for divine intervention.

Practical Guidance for Leaders

- **Expect Defensive Reactions:** Especially around wealth, inclusion, and accountability. Acknowledge resistance rather than dismissing it, but don't dilute Jesus's challenging message.

- **Use Willimon's Humor:** His self-deprecating stories and pastoral honesty can help defuse tension while maintaining theological integrity.

- **Focus on God's Character:** When discussions become overly focused on human behavior, redirect to what the parable reveals about God.

- **Embrace the Riddles:** Don't feel pressured to solve every interpretive puzzle. Sometimes the questions are more important than the answers.

- **Connect to the Table:** Remember that all these parables lead to Jesus's Last Supper. Help participants see how each story prepares us to receive his radical hospitality.

A Pastor's Encouragement

Leading this study means walking with Jesus toward his cross and resurrection. The parables Willimon explores aren't comfortable, but they're transformative. As he reminds us, Jesus "refuses to be refused," and these stories reveal a God whose love is more persistent, more scandalous, and more hopeful than we dare imagine.

Thank you for your willingness to guide others through these challenging conversations. May you and your group discover that the table Jesus sets has room for everyone—including those of us who sometimes find his invitation more disturbing than comforting. In the end, that's exactly why we need to hear his riddles and accept his invitation to "sit for story time" with the one who becomes both our host and our meal.

The journey to the cross leads through the upper room. Jesus is waiting at the table.

Session 1

INTRODUCTION; SOWING, SEEKING, FINDING

Session Goals

This session's reading, reflection, discussion, and prayer will help participants:

+ understand Jesus's "political" intentions from his Palm Sunday entrance to Jerusalem,

+ explore how parables function as riddles that reveal God's kingdom rather than simple moral lessons,

+ examine the parable of the Sower and consider our resistance to God's "recklessly scattered" word,

+ wrestle with the radical hospitality demonstrated in the good Samaritan parable, and

+ recognize that salvation comes through God's initiative, not our achievement.

Biblical Foundations

[Jesus said,] "A farmer went out to scatter his seed. As he was scattering it, some fell on the path where it was crushed, and the birds in the sky came and ate it. Other seed fell on rock. As it grew, it dried up because it had no moisture. Other seed fell among thorny plants. The thorns grew with the plants and choked them. Still other seed landed on good soil. When it grew, it produced one hundred times more grain than was scattered." As he said this, he called out, "Everyone who has ears should pay attention."

Luke 8:5-8

Jesus replied, "A man went down from Jerusalem to Jericho. He encountered thieves, who stripped him naked, beat him up, and left him near death. Now it just so happened that a priest was also going down the same road. When he saw the injured man, he crossed over to the other side of the road and went on his way. Likewise, a Levite came by that spot, saw the injured man, and crossed over to the other side of the road and went on his way. A Samaritan, who was on a journey, came to where the man was. But when he saw him, he was moved with compassion. The Samaritan went to him and bandaged his wounds, tending them with oil and wine. Then he placed the wounded man on his own donkey, took him to an inn, and took care of him. The next day, he took two full days' worth of wages and gave them to the innkeeper. He said, 'Take care of him, and when I return, I will pay you back for any additional costs.'"

Luke 10:30-35

Before Your Session

+ Carefully and prayerfully read the introduction and chapter 1 of *The Last Supper* more than once. Pay attention to Willimon's characteristic blend of humor and theological challenge.
+ Note Willimon's warning that Jesus's parables are "primarily stories about God" rather than moral instruction manuals for us. Prepare yourself to guide discussion away from "what should we do" toward "who is God and what is God up to."

- You will need: Bibles for participants or screen slides prepared with scripture texts, or both; newsprint or a markerboard and markers (for in-person sessions); paper and pens or pencils.
- If using DVD or streaming video, preview the session 1 video segment. Choose the best time in your session plan for viewing it.
- Prepare to be surprised by participant resistance to some of Jesus's more challenging stories. As Willimon notes, we often come to church seeking confirmation of what we already know rather than transformation.

Starting Your Session

Welcome participants. Express your enthusiasm for this Lenten journey with Jesus, but also acknowledge that Willimon warns us we're in for some challenging conversations. These aren't bedtime stories; they're "riddles" that may leave us more puzzled than comforted.

Ask participants to share briefly:

- What's your experience with Palm Sunday? Do you see it as triumphant or ominous?
- When you hear the word *parable*, what comes to mind? Gentle moral lessons or something more disruptive?

Read aloud from Willimon's introduction: "We wanted him to unfurl a battle flag, storm Jerusalem, and set up a new messianic King of David government. Instead, he gave us a simple supper of bread and wine with a bunch of disappointing, simpleton disciples."

Discuss:

- How does this description challenge our expectations of what Jesus should have done?
- What does it mean that Jesus chose a meal over a military campaign?

Opening Prayer

Almighty God, you sent your Son to us not with armies and battle flags, but riding on a borrowed donkey, telling stories that turn our world upside down. As we begin this journey toward his table, give us courage to hear his riddles, wisdom to see his kingdom breaking out among us, and grace to join his work in the world, even when we don't fully understand where he's leading us. **Amen.**

Watch Session Video

Watch the session 1 video segment, "The Reckless Sower," together. Discuss:

+ Which of Willimon's insights most challenged or intrigued you? Why?
+ What questions does this video raise for you about Jesus's storytelling method?

Jesus the Riddler

Read aloud from Willimon: "Matthew and Mark say Jesus said nothing except in parables. . . . Over half of everything Luke quotes from Jesus is in parables or, as we'll name some of them, riddles."

Ask participants:

+ Why might Jesus choose riddles rather than straightforward teaching?
+ What's the difference between a parable and a simple moral lesson?

Read the ancient riddle Willimon mentions: "What building do you enter blind and exit sighted?" (*Answer:* "A school.")

Discuss:

+ How might Jesus's parables function like riddles—requiring us to work for understanding?

+ When has a Bible story or sermon left you more puzzled than when you started? What happened with that confusion over time?

Read aloud Willimon's warning: "God's realm is so different from our kingdoms that when Jesus is revealing, sometimes it feels like he's concealing."

The Sloppy Sower

Recruit a volunteer to read aloud Luke 8:5-8. Then read Jesus's explanation in Luke 8:11-15.

Lead discussion using Willimon's framework:

+ What farmer would actually sow seed this carelessly—throwing it on roads, rocks, and weeds?
+ Willimon asks: "Can you guess why the Sower is most preachers' favorite parable?" What do you think he means?
+ How do the "concerns, riches, and pleasures of life" choke out God's word? Are these necessarily bad things?

Read aloud Willimon's insight: "The Sower just loves to sow, slinging seed with abandon, casting good seed into seemingly hopeless contexts, undeterred by the prospect of farming failure, focusing upon the seed that bears fruit rather than the seed that fails."

Discuss:

+ How does this change your perspective on "failed" evangelism or ministry efforts?
+ When have you seen God's "reckless sowing" produce unexpected fruit?
+ How does your church practice "reckless sowing" versus careful, targeted ministry?

Share Willimon's story about the young man at the rock concert who heard just the word "Why?" and how that led to his return to faith.

Ask:

+ When has God's word reached you through unlikely or "wasteful" circumstances?
+ How does knowing God is the "reckless sower" change how we should approach sharing our faith?

The Impossible Neighbor

Recruit volunteers to read aloud Luke 10:25-37, with different people taking the roles of narrator, lawyer, and Jesus.

+ Why does Jesus make a Samaritan the hero of this story? How would that have landed with Jesus's original audience?
+ Willimon emphasizes the Samaritan's *extravagance*—"two full days' worth of wages" plus a blank check for future costs. Why does this matter?
+ How is this story "more than an example story that exhorts us to better human behavior"?

Read aloud Willimon's interpretation: "Maybe I'm more the good-as-dead, helpless, needy guy down in the ditch than I like to admit, in need of some Samaritan who doesn't mind getting down and dirty with the likes of me."

Ask:

+ When have you been the person in the ditch rather than the helper?
+ How does seeing ourselves as the victim rather than the hero change this parable?
+ Willimon suggests we ask not "To whom should I be neighborly?" but "Who has been neighborly to me?" How does this reframe the story?

Share Willimon's reflection on growing up in segregated South Carolina: "I'm grateful that, in my youth, a number of courageous, caring,

17

reckless Black Christians were merciful good Samaritans to me . . . so that I was saved, lifted out of the ditch of white racism where I lay dying, even though I didn't even know I was sick."

Discuss:

+ How has someone from an unexpected group been a "good Samaritan" to you or your community?
+ What "ditches" might your congregation be lying in without realizing it?

Scripture as GPS

Read aloud Willimon's description of parables as "a GPS taking you to a new world that's God's rather than the fake world in which we bedded down."

Ask:

+ How do these parables challenge our assumptions about how the world works?
+ What "fake world" assumptions do we need to abandon to follow Jesus?

Refer to Willimon's discussion of Simon the Pharisee's dinner party and the "woman of the city" who anointed Jesus's feet (Luke 7:36-50).

Discuss:

+ Why does Jesus tell the parable of the forgiven debtors in response to Simon's judgment?
+ How does this story illustrate that attentiveness to God will produce attentiveness to our neighbors?

Closing Your Session

Final Challenge

Read aloud Willimon's challenge: "'Go and do likewise,'" suggests that this parable has missional intent. God has elected the church to embody

God's gracious intentions beyond the bounds of the church. We can't be faithful just hanging around the church; we've got to be out and about on the road."

Ask participants to take their "seeds" with them as a reminder that they are part of God's "reckless sowing" operation. Challenge them this week to look for one opportunity to be extravagantly gracious—like the good Samaritan—to someone in need.

Use Willimon's discussion questions for final reflection:

+ Has there been a time in your life when you've felt God reaching toward you, slinging seed your way?
+ When's the last time you've been surprised by an unexpected neighbor who was merciful to you?
+ What hinders your church from more actively obeying Jesus's command to "Go! Do!"?

Closing Prayer

Reckless, seed-slinging God, you refuse to give up on any of us, casting your grace into the most unlikely places—including our hearts. Thank you for the good Samaritans you've sent our way when we were lying helpless in life's ditches. Give us eyes to see where you're already at work in our community, courage to join your mission of extravagant mercy, and faith to trust that your "wasteful" love will bear fruit in ways we cannot imagine. As we walk toward your table this Lenten season, help us to scatter seeds of your kingdom with the same reckless abandon that you show toward us. **Amen.**

Session 2
OPEN INVITATION

Session Goals

This session's reading, reflection, discussion, and prayer will help participants:

+ examine Jesus's radical table fellowship and what it reveals about God's kingdom,
+ understand the scandal of God's inclusive invitation to unlikely guests,
+ explore our "good" excuses for avoiding God's party and what they cost us,
+ consider what "There's still room" means for the church's evangelistic calling, and
+ wrestle with Jesus's instructions about dinner party guest lists and their implications for Christian hospitality.

Biblical Foundations

When Jesus noticed how the guests sought out the best seats at the table, he told them a parable. "When someone invites you to a wedding celebration, don't take your seat in the place of honor. Someone more highly regarded than you could have been invited by your host. The host who invited both of you will come and say to you, 'Give your seat to this other person.' Embarrassed, you will take your seat in the least important place. Instead, when you receive an invitation, go and sit in the least important place. When your host approaches you, he will say, 'Friend, move up here to a better seat.' Then you will be honored in the presence of all your fellow guests. All who lift themselves up will be brought low, and those who make themselves low will be lifted up."

Luke 14:7-11

[Jesus said,] "Instead, when you give a banquet, invite the poor, crippled, lame, and blind. And you will be blessed because they can't repay you. Instead, you will be repaid when the just are resurrected."

Luke 14:13-14

Jesus replied, "A certain man hosted a large dinner and invited many people. When it was time for the dinner to begin, he sent his servant to tell the invited guests, 'Come! The dinner is now ready.' One by one, they all began to make excuses. The first one told him, 'I bought a farm and must go and see it. Please excuse me.' Another said, 'I bought five teams of oxen, and I'm going to check on them. Please excuse me.' Another said, 'I just got married, so I can't come.'"

Luke 14:16-20

Before Your Session

+ Carefully and prayerfully read chapter 2 of *The Last Supper* more than once. Pay attention to Willimon's challenge to our "normal" understanding of hospitality and success.
+ Note Willimon's observation that Jesus doesn't just invite the poor—he tells us to invite them. Prepare to discuss the difference between charity and justice, between helping and including.
+ Be prepared for resistance to Jesus's teachings about wealth and social status. Willimon is honest about his own defensiveness; model that honesty for your group.

+ You will need: Bibles for participants, newsprint or markerboard, paper and pens; optional: magazines or newspapers for the closing activity.
+ Review Willimon's story about the disheveled man at his church door and his own lack of graciousness. Consider sharing a similar story from your own experience.

Starting Your Session

+ Welcome participants. Begin by acknowledging that this week's reading may have made some people uncomfortable—as Willimon notes, Jesus has a way of "trashing" our dinner parties.

Ask:

+ What's the most awkward dinner party or social gathering you've ever attended? What made it uncomfortable?
+ When have you felt like an outsider at a social event? When have you felt like an insider?

Read aloud Willimon's scene-setting: "Simon the Pharisee—a pious, biblically knowledgeable religious leader—invited Jesus to dinner. . . . In the Gospels, Pharisees like Simon are depicted as religious experts who can't stand Jesus; yet they persist in inviting him into their homes for supper!"

Discuss:

+ Why do you think religious leaders kept inviting Jesus to dinner, knowing he might disrupt things?
+ When has Jesus "disrupted" your comfortable assumptions about faith or church?

Opening Prayer

Generous God, you have set a table with room for everyone, yet we often prefer our exclusive dinner parties with people just like us. As we explore your radical hospitality today, help us see our world through your eyes—where the hungry are filled and the proud are sent away empty-handed. Give us courage to examine our own excuses and wisdom to recognize the feast you're already preparing. **Amen.**

Watch Session Video

Watch the session 2 video segment, "There's Still Room," together. Discuss:

+ Which of Willimon's insights about God's "open table" most challenged you?
+ How do you respond to his claim that Jesus's dinner party instructions aren't just suggestions but "direct instruction on how to live your way into the practical ethics of the kingdom"?

Jesus Crashes the Dinner Party

Recruit three volunteers to read Luke 14:1-6 (the healing on the Sabbath), Luke 14:7-11 (table etiquette), and Luke 14:12-14 (guest list instructions).

After each reading, discuss using Willimon's framework:

The Sabbath Healing (vv. 1-6)

+ Why does Jesus heal the man with "abnormal body swelling" right in the middle of a dinner party?
+ Willimon notes that Jesus turns the dining room into a hospital. When have you seen the church prioritize human need over social propriety?

Table Etiquette (vv. 7-11)

+ How is Jesus's advice about seating different from typical social climbing strategies?
+ What does "All who lift themselves up will be brought low" mean in practical terms?

The Guest List (vv. 12-14)

Read aloud Willimon's paraphrase of Jesus's instructions: "Don't invite your buddies at the club, the few family members who still speak to you, or your fat-cat neighbors. . . . Instead, when you give a banquet, invite the poor, crippled, lame, and blind; they'll never repay."

Ask:

+ How does this challenge our normal understanding of networking and reciprocal social relationships?
+ What would it look like for your church to follow these instructions literally?

The Absurd Excuses

Have volunteers read Luke 14:15-24, the parable of the Great Banquet. Before discussion, read Willimon's analysis of the excuses:

+ "In a region where arable land is scarce, this guy has bought a farm and hasn't seen it?"
+ "A farmer purchased costly farm animals before checking them out?"
+ "A patriarchal Near Eastern male lets a wife keep him from a huge banquet?"

Ask:

+ What makes these excuses so absurd? What makes them so familiar?
+ Willimon notes that the things that keep people from the banquet aren't evil things—they're "concerns, riches, and pleasures of life." How do good things become barriers to God's kingdom?

Read Willimon's observation: "Is providing for the well-being of your family not a good thing? Taking care of business is what businesspeople are

supposed to do. Don't we believe that sacrificing your social life for your marriage and family is a great virtue?"

Discuss:

+ When have good priorities become excuses for avoiding God's call?
+ What are the most common "good excuses" people give for not engaging more deeply in church or faith?

"There's Still Room"

Focus on the master's response to the refusals in Luke 14:21-23.

Read aloud Willimon's key insight: "I want you to take 'there is still room' as the key to this Big Banquet riddle."

Ask:

+ How does knowing "there's still room" change your perspective on evangelism?
+ Willimon says the host "won't rest until everybody in town is at the table." How does this challenge our assumptions about who belongs in church?

Share Willimon's John Wesley quote: "'Salvation for all!' cried out John Wesley in the fields and alleyways of England, obedient to Christ's command, 'Go to the highways and back alleys and urge people to come in so that my house will be filled.'"

Discuss:

+ The median age in many denominations is rising rapidly. How does this parable speak to that reality?
+ What would it look like for your church to be actively "out on the highways and back alleys" with invitations?

Today's Feast

Read Willimon's crucial insight: "In Jesus's parable of the Great Banquet, the invitation isn't just to some future heavenly feast, it's also to a meal that's in session this very moment, if we just have the eyes to see."

Ask:

+ Where do you see God's kingdom banquet happening now?
+ How is your church a "local rendition of Jesus's table fellowship"?

Share Willimon's challenge: "Don't waste your time looking for kingdom outbreak on the floor of the US Senate, or at the Pentagon, much less at a state dinner at the White House. Look local: your kitchen table that you've opened to someone who didn't think they belonged, potluck suppers in the church basement for people who had never set foot in a church, at the Lord's Table next Sunday."

Discuss:

+ When has your congregation experienced something like this "kingdom outbreak"?
+ What prevents us from seeing ordinary church meals as part of God's great banquet?

The Uncomfortable Truth About Invitation

Read Willimon's pastoral honesty: "If you've never been excluded from a party, rented a tux only to find that your invitation got lost in the mail, been turned away at the door because your name is not on the list, or on the other hand, if you've never been surprised by an invitation to the biggest bash this town's ever seen, even when you didn't expect to make the cut, then I'm unsure if I'm a good enough preacher to explain this parable to you."

Ask:

+ When have you been unexpectedly excluded? Unexpectedly included?
+ How do these experiences help us understand God's grace?

Discuss Willimon's observation about our tendency to take credit: "Listen to us trying to take credit for our being at the Lord's Table: 'Since I've accepted Jesus as my Savior,' 'Now that I've taken Jesus into my heart.' Or 'Since I gave my life to Christ.' Note the preponderance of the first-person singular."

Ask:

+ How does this parable challenge our "personal savior" language?
+ What difference does it make to know we're at God's table only by invitation?

Closing Your Session

Willimon's Challenge

Read aloud: "Any church that's not actively out on the 'highways and back alleys' delivering the message ('Hey, there's still room.') is not yet fully a church."

Ask participants to consider:

+ What is one specific way you could extend God's invitation this week—whether to church, to your table, or simply to belonging?
+ How might your congregation become more intentional about delivering the "there's still room" message?

Use Willimon's discussion questions:

+ What's your earliest memory of your awareness that, for you, "There's still room"?

+ What do you think ought to happen in your congregation for your church to more closely resemble Jesus's expansive invitation to his banquet?

Closing Prayer

Gracious Host, you have prepared a feast with room for everyone, yet we often act like bouncers at an exclusive club. Forgive our excuses and our exclusions. Help us trust that your table is big enough for the people we find difficult, different, or disappointing—including ourselves. This week, make us bold ambassadors of your "there's still room" invitation, and help us see our own meals and gatherings as extensions of your great banquet. Give us eyes to recognize the kingdom feast that's already underway and hearts courageous enough to join the party. **Amen.**

Session 3
FEASTING WITH THE FOUND

Session Goals

This session's reading, reflection, discussion, and prayer will help participants:

+ recognize themselves in both the prodigal son and the grumbling older brother;

+ understand God as the "prodigally gracious" father who throws expensive parties for undeserving children;

+ explore the church's calling to seek, find, and celebrate the lost with God;

+ address the scandal of grace for the "undeserving" and our resistance to it;

+ examine how these parables reveal God's character rather than human morality; and

+ consider the missional implications of God's relentless searching.

Biblical Foundations

Jesus told them this parable: "Suppose someone among you had one hundred sheep and lost one of them. Wouldn't he leave the other ninety-nine in the pasture and search for the lost one until he finds it? And when he finds it, he is thrilled and places it on his shoulders. When he arrives home, he calls together his friends and neighbors, saying to them, 'Celebrate with me because I've found my lost sheep.'"

Luke 15:3-6

[Jesus told them,] "Or what woman, if she owns ten silver coins and loses one of them, won't light a lamp and sweep the house, searching her home carefully until she finds it? When she finds it, she calls together her friends and neighbors, saying, 'Celebrate with me because I've found my lost coin.'"

Luke 15:8-9

[Jesus told them,] "So he got up and went to his father.

While he was still a long way off, his father saw him and was moved with compassion. His father ran to him, hugged him, and kissed him. Then his son said, 'Father, I have sinned against heaven and against you. I no longer deserve to be called your son.' But the father said to his servants, 'Quickly, bring out the best robe and put it on him! Put a ring on his finger and sandals on his feet!'"

Luke 15:20-22

Before Your Session

+ Carefully and prayerfully read chapter 3 of *The Last Supper* more than once. Pay special attention to Willimon's insistence that these are "stories about God" rather than moral lessons about us.
+ Note Willimon's challenging statement: "The parables almost always and everywhere speak about God. Who is God? What is God up to?" Prepare to redirect discussion away from "What should we do?" toward "Who is God?"

+ Be ready to address the discomfort many feel with God's "unfair" grace. Willimon acknowledges this directly: "Grace for me is good but when it's grace for you, considering how suspect your repentance is when compared with mine, then sometimes grace doesn't feel so amazing."

+ Consider sharing your own experience of being either the younger or older brother—or both at different times.

+ You will need: Bibles, newsprint or markerboard, colored pencils or markers, small stones or coins for the closing activity.

Starting Your Session

Welcome participants. Acknowledge that this session deals with some of Jesus's most beloved—and most disturbing—stories.

Begin with this scenario: "Imagine your church's biggest donor announces they're leaving all their money to the church when they die. But then their estranged child—who hasn't been to church in twenty years and has a reputation for wild living—shows up on their deathbed, and the donor decides to throw a huge welcome-home party instead."

Ask:

+ How would your congregation react?

+ Who would you identify with in that scenario?

Read aloud the context from Luke 15:1-2: "All the tax collectors and sinners were gathering around Jesus to listen to him. The Pharisees and legal experts were grumbling, saying, 'This man welcomes sinners and eats with them.'"

Discuss:

+ The religious leaders don't criticize Jesus's theology—they grumble about his dinner companions. Why does this matter?

+ When has your church grumbled about who Jesus welcomes?

Opening Prayer

Searching God, you leave the safety of the ninety-nine to find the one, tear up the house looking for what's lost, and throw expensive parties for children who don't deserve them. Help us today to see ourselves honestly in these stories—sometimes lost, sometimes found, sometimes grateful, sometimes grumbling. Open our hearts to the scandalous mathematics of your grace and our calling to join your search-and-rescue mission. **Amen.**

Watch Session Video

Watch the session 3 video segment, "The Wasteful Father," together. Discuss:

+ How does Willimon's interpretation challenge your previous understanding of these familiar parables?
+ What did you think about his emphasis on God's "horrible home economics"?

The Reckless Shepherd

Read Luke 15:3-7, then discuss using Willimon's framework:

Read aloud his analysis: "Which one of you wouldn't do that? People are rolling in the aisles with laughter. 'Tell us another one, Jesus,' they hoot."

Ask:

+ What's so absurd about this shepherd's behavior?
+ Willimon says this sloppy Sower has "switched jobs" to become a reckless shepherd. What does this tell us about God's character?

Note Willimon's crucial insight: "These are not stories about us. These are stories about God."

Discuss:

+ How does knowing this is about God change how you hear the story?

+ What does it mean that God practices "scandalous shepherding"?

The House-Wrecking Woman

Read Luke 15:8-10, using Willimon's vivid retelling.

Read aloud: "Which one of you wouldn't do that? Nobody would act like that. None of us would engage in such horrible home economics . . . much less throw an expensive party for a trifle like one recovered sheep or a single small coin retrieved. None of us."

Ask:

+ Why does the woman's behavior seem so excessive for finding one coin?
+ What does this story reveal about what God considers valuable?

Emphasize Willimon's theological point: "God's kingdom accounting is different from what counts in our kingdoms."

Discuss:

+ How does God's "accounting" differ from the world's?
+ When have you seen the church value what the world considers worthless?

The Most Wonderful Word

Share Willimon's childhood memory: "Though I was a child when I heard it, I still remember our pastor's sermon, 'The Most Wonderful, Comforting Word in the Bible.' The word? It's prominent in these two stories: until."

Ask:

+ When does God call off the search for the lost?
+ How does the word *until* change your understanding of God's persistence?

Read the litany of questions Willimon poses: "When a person blasphemes . . . When someone dies without having accepted God's invitation? If a miscreant commits an act so irredeemably horrible . . . Hitler? Stalin?"

Discuss:

+ What are the limits of God's searching love?
+ How do we balance God's persistence with human responsibility?

The Prodigal Father

Have volunteers read Luke 15:11-32, with different people taking the roles of narrator, younger son, father, and older brother.

Before discussion, read Willimon's reframing: "I know you're accustomed to calling this the prodigal (wasteful, extravagant, loose living) son but will you agree that the most interesting character in the story is the prodigally gracious, welcoming father?"

Focus on the Father's Response: Read Willimon's description: "The father doesn't give a rip for contrite speeches. 'Save the Repentance Drama for your application to Law School. You wanted a party? I'll show you a party.'"

Ask:

+ Why doesn't the father want to hear the son's carefully prepared apology?
+ What does the father's interruption teach us about grace?

Discuss Willimon's observation: "What we wanted was for the father to receive the boy back home. . . . Then there's supposed to be an unsmiling lecture. . . . What we get is the father's extravagant (might I say, wasteful, prodigal) unconditional party."

Ask:

+ Why are we more comfortable with lectures than parties?
+ When has God surprised you with celebration instead of scolding?

Meeting the Older Brother

Focus on Luke 15:25-32 and the older brother's response.

Read Willimon's analysis: "The older brother's grumbling reminds us of the griping of the Pharisees that occasioned this parable. We got here first. We've sat through years of boring Bible studies and engaged in Lenten self-denial practices . . . "

Ask:

+ When do you identify with the older brother?
+ What makes his complaints seem reasonable?

Share Willimon's story about the pastor who reached out to people "in the piney woods beyond the train tracks" and baptized four people but lost five church members who said, "We don't want to go to church with a bunch of crackheads and their kids."

Discuss:

+ How does this story illuminate the older brother's mindset?
+ When has your church struggled with welcoming "those people"?

Read Willimon's confession: "I have met the grumbling, stuffy older brother: me."

Ask:

+ How can church leaders like you avoid becoming older brothers?
+ What's the difference between faithful church membership and older brother syndrome?

The Church as Search Party

Read Willimon's missional conclusion: "Our duty as citizens of God's kingdom? Search. Find. Forgive. Celebrate. Repeat."

Share his story about the young pastor who started "knocking on the doors of our neighbors" and saw attendance nearly double, plus the pastor

who hung out in bars because "if you want me to stay away from that place, you are going to figure out how to keep Jesus out of that bar."

Ask:

+ How is your church joining Jesus in seeking out, searching for, and saving the lost?
+ Where might Jesus already be at work in your community that you haven't noticed?

Discuss Willimon's challenge: "The evangelistic, missional question is, Will we?"

Closing Your Session

The Search Party Commission

Read aloud Willimon's ending: "At the end of Luke's Gospel the risen Christ, teller of these tales, commissions his followers, all of them, to be evangelists. It's our job to tell 'all nations' the good news of a feast that begins with 'a change of heart and life for the forgiveness of sins.' . . . He calls us 'witnesses,' making each of us into servants who deliver the Master's invitation to the feast, sowers who sling the seed, shepherds who seek a lost sheep, women who search for a lost coin, those who open the door and say, 'This feast is for you.'"

Challenge participants:

+ Keep your stone/coin as a reminder that you are part of God's search-and-rescue operation.
+ This week, look for one opportunity to be part of finding someone who feels lost.
+ Practice celebrating rather than lecturing when you encounter grace in action.

Use Willimon's discussion questions:

+ Be honest, do you think you would be among the celebrators, or would you be a grumbler outside the party for the homecoming of the prodigal son?
+ How's your church joining with Jesus in seeking out, searching for, and saving the lost?

Closing Prayer

Prodigally gracious God, you practice horrible home economics, leaving the ninety-nine to search for the one, throwing expensive parties for children who squander your gifts. Help us trust your wasteful love even when it offends our sense of fairness. Make us partners in your search-and-rescue mission, willing to tear up our comfort zones to find the lost. Give us the father's eyes that watch the horizon for returning children, and save us from the older brother's spirit that would rather be right than celebrate. As we continue toward your table, help us remember that we are there only because you searched for us first. **Amen.**

Session 4
CRUMBS FROM THE TABLE

Session Goals

This session's reading, reflection, discussion, and prayer will help participants:

+ confront Jesus's consistent and uncomfortable teachings about wealth and poverty,

+ examine the blindness that privilege can create and the responsibility that comes with resources,

+ understand the parable of Lazarus and the Rich Man as both warning and gospel,

+ consider Zacchaeus as a model of how the wealthy can respond to Jesus's salvation,

+ wrestle with the difference between charity and justice in Christian discipleship, and

+ address defensive responses to Jesus's economic teachings while maintaining his clear message.

Biblical Foundations

[Jesus said,] "There was a certain rich man who clothed himself in purple and fine linen, and who feasted luxuriously every day. At his gate lay a certain poor man named Lazarus who was covered with sores. Lazarus longed to eat the crumbs that fell from the rich man's table. Instead, dogs would come and lick his sores."

"The poor man died and was carried by angels to Abraham's side. The rich man also died and was buried. While being tormented in the place of the dead, he looked up and saw Abraham at a distance with Lazarus at his side."

Luke 16:19-23

[God said,] "Child, remember that during your lifetime you received good things, whereas Lazarus received terrible things. Now Lazarus is being comforted and you are in great pain. Moreover, a great crevasse has been fixed between us and you."

Luke 16:25-26

When Jesus came to that spot, he looked up and said, "Zacchaeus, come down at once. I must stay in your home today." So Zacchaeus came down at once, happy to welcome Jesus.

Everyone who saw this grumbled, saying, "He has gone to be the guest of a sinner."

Zacchaeus stopped and said to the Lord, "Look, Lord, I give half of my possessions to the poor. And if I have cheated anyone, I repay them four times as much."

Jesus said to him, "Today, salvation has come to this household because he too is a son of Abraham."

Luke 19:5-9

Before Your Session

+ Read chapter 4 carefully, noting Willimon's honest admission of his own defensiveness about wealth. Model this honesty for your group.

+ Be prepared for significant resistance to this session's content. Willimon acknowledges: "If that's your expectation for sermons or your idea of church, then the riddles of Jesus will sound strange."
+ Note that this may be the most difficult session for many participants. Willimon admits he has "never had to worry where my children's next meal came from" and lives "a long way from the Lazaruses of Durham."
+ Consider your own congregation's economic makeup and prepare to address defensiveness constructively.
+ You will need: Bibles, newsprint or markerboard, paper and pens, optional: newspapers or magazines showing wealth/poverty contrasts.

Starting Your Session

Welcome participants. Acknowledge that this session deals with some of Jesus's most challenging teachings—ones that many of us would prefer to avoid.

Begin with this reality check: "Willimon notes that this parable 'rarely makes our Top Ten lists of Jesus's stories.' Why do you think that is?"

Share this statistic from Willimon: "I listened to over a hundred video sermons preached in that congregation. Not one word from their pulpit on the two thousand verses in Scripture on the evil of riches."

Ask:

+ Why might churches avoid preaching about wealth and poverty?
+ What's your gut reaction when money becomes the topic in church?

Read aloud Willimon's honest confession: "Because of my economic circumstances, this story sounds like bad news. I've preached sermons on this text, but it took a lot of fancy interpretive footwork for me to do so."

Discuss:

+ How do you respond to Willimon's honesty about his own defensiveness?
+ When have you found yourself making "interpretive footwork" to avoid difficult biblical teachings?

Opening Prayer

Holy God, your word cuts through our comfortable assumptions and challenges our priorities. As we wrestle today with Jesus' hard teachings about wealth and poverty, help us see clearly—both the world's need and our own responsibility. Give us courage to face uncomfortable truths about ourselves and our society, and wisdom to respond with both justice and grace. Open our eyes to see Lazarus at our own gates. **Amen.**

Watch Session Video

Watch the session 4 video segment, "The Rich Man's Hell," together. Discuss:

+ How did Willimon's interpretation of these economic parables challenge your previous understanding?
+ What was your reaction to his statement that "Jesus takes sides" in economic matters?

Setting the Scene: A Tale of Two Tables

Read Luke 16:19-21, noting Willimon's vivid details about the contrast between the rich man's daily feasting and Lazarus's desperate hunger.

Point out Willimon's observations:

+ The rich man is nameless ("if you've met one of these fat-cats, you've met them all")

+ Lazarus is the only person in all the parables who gets a name ("One whom God helps")
+ "Feasted luxuriously" uses the same Greek word as the celebration in the Prodigal Son parable

Ask:

+ Why does it matter that the poor man has a name while the rich man doesn't?
+ How does the detail about daily feasting versus occasional celebration change the story's impact?

Read Willimon's description: "Eighty-five of the richest people in the world own as much as the poorest 3.5 billion people. The six heirs to Wal-Mart have more money than the poorest 48.8 million American families put together. And you thought that the Bible is irrelevant to our contemporary world!"

Discuss:

+ How does this description help us understand the parable's relevance?
+ What "gates" separate rich and poor in our community?

The Problem of Sight

Focus on Willimon's key insight: "The rich man had the opportunity to help. Yet his lifestyle has made Lazarus invisible. He doesn't oppress or abuse Lazarus. He simply never sees him."

Compare this to earlier parables where vision was crucial:

+ "Do you see this woman?" (Luke 7:44)
+ The Samaritan "saw him" and stopped to help
+ The father "saw him" while the son was still far off

Ask:

+ How does wealth create blindness?
+ When have you realized you weren't "seeing" someone in need?
+ What makes people invisible in our society?

Read Willimon's practical advice: "If you want to avoid the claim of those on the sidewalk begging you for a handout, take care not to look at their eyes."

Discuss:

+ How do we protect ourselves from seeing need?
+ What would it mean for your church to truly "see" the Lazarus figures in your community?

The Great Reversal

Read Luke 16:22-26, focusing on the dramatic role reversal in the afterlife.

Note Willimon's interpretation: "The main characteristic of eternity: The life to come will be a dramatic turning of the tables for the rich and the poor."

Read Abraham's explanation: "Child, remember that during your lifetime you received good things, whereas Lazarus received terrible things. Now Lazarus is being comforted and you are in great pain."

Ask:

+ How does this reversal challenge our assumptions about success and blessing?
+ What does it mean that the rich man's riches gave him "heaven on earth"?
+ How do we reconcile God's love with this stark judgment?

Discuss Willimon's insight: "The gate, your fancy security system by which you lock out the poor, has become your prison."

Handling Defensive Reactions

Read aloud Willimon's anticipation of resistance: "Sorry if you are uncomfortable with criticism of the wealthiest 1 percent, or if you smell some sort of socialist class-conflict being fomented here."

Address common defensive responses Willimon mentions:

+ "Programs for the poor just won't work,"
+ "The welfare system is broken,"
+ "It sounds downright Socialist."

Read Willimon's response: "Tell it to Jesus. He thinks he's talking about the 'real world,' that is, the world as God intends it to be."

Ask:

+ How do we distinguish between Jesus's teachings and our political positions?
+ What's the difference between critiquing systems and taking partisan stands?
+ How can the church address economic justice without becoming a political organization?

Good News for Whom?

Address Willimon's crucial question: Who hears this as good news?

Read his reflection: "I'm defensive because I assume that there's nobody reading this book who would hear Jesus's story as anything but judgment, condemnation, and bad news. But if you are one of those who is often absent from or invisible to our affluent congregations, that is, somebody who can relate to how it feels to be Lazarus, then this story's for you."

Ask:

+ For whom is this parable good news?
+ How does the gospel include both comfort and challenge?

+ What would it mean for our church to be good news for both rich and poor?

Zacchaeus: A Different Model

Transition to Luke 19:1-10, noting the contrast between the rich man's blindness and Zacchaeus's transformation.

Read Willimon's surprise: "Bypassing all the humble, down-to-earth folks serving or being served at the church soup kitchen, Jesus invites himself to the home of the richest oligarch in town."

Emphasize the key difference: "Once lunch is served, before Jesus has a chance to say anything, lay out his program, or tell any of his notorious stories, Zacchaeus taps his Irish lead crystal goblet to propose a toast: 'Look, Lord! I give half of my possessions to the poor. And if I have cheated anyone, I repay them four times as much.'"

Ask:

+ What enabled Zacchaeus to respond so differently from the rich man in the parable?
+ How does Zacchaeus model faithful wealth stewardship?
+ What does Jesus's definition of salvation ("Today salvation has come to this household") tell us?

Note Willimon's insight: "Salvation is an undeserved, unearned, unmerited gift and also a life-changing, costly assignment."

Closing Your Session

The Lazarus Challenge

Read Willimon's practical challenge: "Good news. You know the truth. It's too late for the rich man in the parable, but it's not too late for you. There's still time to live the truth rather than the lie that masquerades as The American Dream."

Ask participants to consider:

- Who is the "Lazarus" in your community whom you haven't been seeing?
- What is one concrete step you could take this week to bridge a gap between rich and poor?
- How might your congregation move beyond charity toward justice?

Use Willimon's discussion questions:

- Your call: Is Jesus's parable of Lazarus and the rich man good news or bad?
- What's one thing your congregation could do to participate more actively in Jesus's ministry to rich and poor?

Closing Prayer

God of justice and mercy, you see every Lazarus lying at our gates and every rich person feasting while others hunger. Forgive our blindness to need and our comfort with inequality. Help us receive your salvation like Zacchaeus—not just as gift but as assignment. Give us courage to examine our own privilege honestly and wisdom to use our resources as faithful stewards. Open our eyes to see, our hearts to care, and our hands to act. As we continue toward your table, remind us that your feast has room for both rich and poor, but only when we learn to see and serve each other. **Amen.**

Session 5
REFUSING
THE HOST

Session Goals

This session's reading, reflection, discussion, and prayer will help participants:

+ understand accountability and stewardship in discipleship through the parable of the Minas,

+ examine our tendency to treat God's gifts as our possessions rather than assignments,

+ explore the violence inherent in rejecting God's messengers through the Wicked Tenants parable,

+ confront the uncomfortable truth about our collective refusal of God's authority,

+ prepare for the ultimate cost of following Jesus to Jerusalem and the cross, and

+ recognize the difference between fearful caution and faithful risk-taking.

Biblical Foundations

He said, "A certain man who was born into royalty went to a distant land to receive his kingdom and then return. He called together ten servants and gave each of them money worth four months' wages. He said, 'Do business with this until I return.' His citizens hated him, so they sent a representative after him who said, 'We don't want this man to be our king.' After receiving his kingdom, he returned and called the servants to whom he had given the money to find out how much they had earned. The first servant came forward and said, 'Your money has earned a return of one thousand percent.' The king replied, 'Excellent! You are a good servant. Because you have been faithful in a small matter, you will have authority over ten cities.'

"The second servant came and said, 'Master, your money has made a return of five hundred percent.' To this one, the king said, 'You will have authority over five cities.'

"Another servant came and said, 'Master, here is your money. I wrapped it up in a scarf for safekeeping. I was afraid of you because you are a stern man. You withdraw what you haven't deposited and you harvest what you haven't planted.' The king replied, 'I will judge you by the words of your own mouth, you worthless servant! You knew, did you, that I'm a stern man, withdrawing what I didn't deposit, and harvesting what I didn't plant?"

Luke 19:12-22

Jesus told the people this parable: "A certain man planted a vineyard, rented it to tenant farmers, and went on a trip for a long time. When it was time, he sent a servant to collect from the tenants his share of the fruit of the vineyard. But the tenants sent him away, beaten and empty-handed. The man sent another servant. But they beat him, treated him disgracefully, and sent him away empty-handed as well. He sent a third servant. They wounded this servant and threw him out. The owner of the vineyard said, 'What should I do? I'll send my son, whom I love dearly. Perhaps they will respect him.' But when they saw him, they said to each other, 'This is the heir. Let's kill him so the inheritance will be ours.' They threw him out of the vineyard and killed him. What will the owner of the vineyard do to them?"

Luke 20:9-15

Before Your Session

+ Carefully read chapter 5, noting Willimon's distinction between the harsh earthly king in the Minas parable and God's character revealed elsewhere.
+ Be prepared to address the violence in both parables. Willimon acknowledges these are stories "so violent we wish Jesus hadn't told them."
+ Note his emphasis that we are not "hard-hearted, active criminals" but rather "unimaginative, risk-averse, fearful folk whose prudence and phobias sometimes get the best of us."
+ Consider your own tendency toward "playing it safe" versus taking faithful risks.
+ You will need: Bibles, newsprint or markerboard, small wrapped items (candy, coins, etc.) for the closing activity.
+ Prepare to discuss current examples of rejecting God's messengers or burying God's gifts.

Starting Your Session

Welcome participants. Note that we're approaching Holy Week in our journey with Jesus, and these parables prepare us for the violence and rejection that awaits.

Begin by asking:

+ What's the difference between being "careful" and being "fearful" when it comes to faith?
+ When have you played it too safe in your Christian life? When have you taken faithful risks?

49

Read aloud Willimon's observation: "We sympathize with the one-mina guy because most of us are not multitalented. Neither are most churches I've served."

Ask:

+ How do you respond to Willimon's honest assessment of limited talents?
+ What does it mean to be faithful stewards when we don't feel particularly gifted?

Opening Prayer

God of generous gifts and high expectations, you entrust us with more than we think we can handle and expect more than we think we can give. As we explore these difficult parables today, help us distinguish between faithful caution and fearful timidity. Give us courage to unwrap the gifts you've given us and wisdom to risk them for your kingdom. Prepare our hearts for the hard truths about our own resistance to your authority. **Amen.**

Watch Session Video

Watch the session 5 video segment, "The Buried Talent," together. Discuss:

+ How did Willimon's interpretation of the "harsh king" versus God's character affect your understanding of the Minas parable?
+ What struck you about his analysis of our tendency to bury God's gifts?

The Parable of the Buried Gift

Read Luke 19:11-27, then discuss Willimon's framework for understanding this difficult parable.

The King's Harshness

Note Willimon's warning: "Unlike many other parables, we must not too quickly assume that this king is God the Father or Jesus the Son. The words 'bring them here and slaughter them in front of me' wouldn't fit in Jesus's mouth."

Ask:

+ How does recognizing this as a critique of worldly kingship change the parable's meaning?
+ What does this story tell us about how earthly power operates versus God's kingdom?

The One-Mina Servant

Read Willimon's sympathetic analysis: "Our sympathies lie with the servant who receives one mina who does what is prudent, responsible, careful, and secure, what any reasonable person would do, that is, what any of us would do."

Focus on the servant's defense: "I was afraid of you because you are a stern man."

Ask:

+ How does fear prevent faithful risk-taking?
+ When has a fear of failure kept you from using your gifts?
+ What's the difference between calling God "stern" and recognizing God's expectations?

The Real King

Contrast this with Willimon's insight: "The king has not taken anything from anybody. On the contrary, he has recklessly given a bunch of money to his servants, sowing among them a huge amount of cash without being asked by them to do so."

Discuss:

+ How is God's generosity different from the harsh king's expectations?
+ What does it mean that God "sows" gifts among us without being asked?
+ How do we confuse God's expectations with worldly demands for performance?

Love as Our One Gift

Read Willimon's crucial insight: "All we've been given is one little mina, I mean, gift: *love*. Repeatedly Jesus stressed, Love one another. . . . Love yourself; love your neighbor. . . . Love your enemies, even. . . . Then he left town. What will we have to show for ourselves when there's an accounting?"

Share his church council story about the homeless people sleeping on the church porch and the member who said: "I don't know just what we ought to do, but I do know that if we make a mistake in what we decide tonight, Jesus commands us to err on the side of love."

Ask:

+ How does reducing our "assignment" to love simplify faithful living?
+ When has your church chosen to "err on the side of love"?
+ What would it look like to invest love recklessly rather than bury it safely?

The Violence of Refusal

Transition to Luke 20:9-19, the parable of the Wicked Tenants.

Read the parable, then note Willimon's historical context using Isaiah 5:1-7.

God's Vineyard

Explain that everyone knew "vineyard" meant Israel, and the owner's repeated sending of servants represented God's long history with the people.

Ask:

+ How does knowing this is about God's relationship with Israel change your reading?
+ What does the escalating violence against the servants tell us about human resistance to God?

The Beloved Son

Focus on Luke 20:13: "I'll send my son, whom I love dearly. Perhaps they will respect him."

Read Willimon's insight: "The parable does not say that the owner of the vineyard actually destroyed the tenants just as the renters murdered the son. The parable says only what—if there's an ounce of justice in this world—should happen."

Ask:

+ Why does the owner keep sending representatives despite the violence?
+ What does sending the beloved son reveal about God's character?
+ How do we act like "wicked tenants" who treat God's world as our possession?

The Modern Vineyard

Read Willimon's contemporary application: "We thought we were so smart, despoiling creation as if it were ours, mining, building, developing, and using and abusing the world as we please. We've got the whole world in our hands."

Share his story about Pleasant Grove church that closed after refusing to welcome a Black family, and the district superintendent's reflection: "God isn't kind to a disobedient church."

Ask:

+ How do we act as if the church belongs to us rather than God?
+ When has your congregation had to choose between comfort and faithfulness?
+ What does it mean that "God isn't kind to a disobedient church"?

The Owner's Response

Read Willimon's crucial question: "What will the owner of the vineyard do to them?"

Note his insight: "What's the Father's response to the long history of refusal and sometimes even violent rejection that God and God's prophets have received from the temporary inhabitants of God's vineyard? Send the beloved Son."

Discuss:

+ How does God's response to rejection differ from what we might expect?
+ What does it mean that Jesus tells this story knowing he's heading toward his own rejection?
+ How does the cross represent both judgment and grace?

Hope in the Owner's Persistence

Read Willimon's conclusion: "The Son, come to Jerusalem to collect God's due, shall, after supper in an upper room, indeed be betrayed with a kiss, beaten, cast out of the city, and murdered by a bunch of temporary tenants who act as if the Holy City belongs to them."

But note his hope: "At the Last Supper on Maundy Thursday, he shall promise—even to those who have routinely misunderstood, disobeyed, and refused—the undeserved gift of God's kingdom."

Ask:

+ How does knowing the end of the story change how we read these violent parables?
+ What hope do we find in God's refusal to be refused?
+ How does the Last Supper represent the owner's ultimate response?

Closing Your Session

Unwrapping Your Gifts

Give each participant a small, wrapped item (candy, coin, etc.). Say: "Willimon reminds us that most of us aren't multitalented, but we've all been given something. These wrapped gifts represent the talents, resources, and opportunities God has entrusted to us."

Ask participants to hold their wrapped gifts and consider:

+ What gifts has God given you that you might be "burying" out of fear or caution?
+ What would it look like to "unwrap" and risk those gifts for God's kingdom this week?
+ How might God be calling you to be less of a "temporary tenant" and more of a faithful steward?

After reflection, invite participants to unwrap their gifts as a symbol of commitment to stop burying what God has given them.

Use Willimon's discussion questions:

+ How have you experienced the dogged determination of Christ to connect with you in spite of your efforts to evade him?
+ Take an honest look at your church and ask, "How have we been ungrateful tenants of God's vineyard?"

Closing Prayer

Persistent God, you keep sending your messengers even when we refuse to listen, keep offering your gifts even when we bury them in fear. Forgive us for acting like owners rather than tenants, for treating your vineyard as our possession. Help us unwrap the gifts you've given us and invest them boldly in your kingdom. As we approach the cross with Jesus, remind us that your love refuses to be refused, and your grace persists even through our rebellion. Make us faithful stewards of all you've entrusted to us. **Amen.**

Session 6
THE HOST WHO BECOMES THE MEAL

Session Goals

This session's reading, reflection, discussion, and prayer will help participants:

+ understand the Last Supper as the culmination of Jesus's table ministry and parable teaching;

+ explore the scandal of Jesus sharing intimate fellowship with his betrayers;

+ connect Maundy Thursday to the Emmaus encounter and the church's ongoing Eucharist;

+ recognize how Jesus's "riddles" are embodied and enacted at the table;

+ consider what it means that Jesus refuses to be refused, even by death; and

+ understand the church as continuation of Jesus's kingdom banquet.

Biblical Foundations

When the time came, Jesus took his place at the table, and the apostles joined him. He said to them, "I have earnestly desired to eat this Passover with you before I suffer. I tell you, I won't eat it until it is fulfilled in God's kingdom. "After taking a cup and giving thanks, he said, "Take this and share it among yourselves. I tell you that from now on I won't drink from the fruit of the vine until God's kingdom has come." After taking the bread and giving thanks, he broke it and gave it to them, saying, "This is my body, which is given for you. Do this in remembrance of me." In the same way, he took the cup after the meal and said, "This cup is the new covenant by my blood, which is poured out for you.

"But look! My betrayer is with me; his hand is on this table."

Luke 22:14-21

But they urged him, saying, "Stay with us. It's nearly evening, and the day is almost over." So he went in to stay with them. After he took his seat at the table with them, he took the bread, blessed and broke it, and gave it to them. Their eyes were opened and they recognized him, but he disappeared from their sight.

Luke 24:29-31

Before Your Session

- Carefully read chapter 6, noting how Willimon brings together all the themes from Jesus's parables into the climactic meal.
- Pay attention to his insight that the Last Supper wasn't the "last" supper after all—it becomes the "first" of many resurrection meals.
- Note his emphasis that the Eucharist is not a "sad memorial meal" but an "Emmaus-inspired victory celebration."
- Be prepared to discuss how the church's table fellowship continues Jesus's radical hospitality.

+ You will need: Bibles, elements for a simple communion service (if appropriate for your tradition), bread and cup for demonstration, newsprint or markerboard.
+ Consider how this session might prepare participants for Maundy Thursday and Easter observances.

Starting Your Session

Welcome participants to this final session of our Lenten journey. Acknowledge that we've arrived at the destination Jesus has been leading us toward all along—his table.

Begin with reflection:

+ What has surprised you most about Jesus's parables during our study?
+ How has your understanding of God's kingdom changed through these "riddles"?

Read aloud Willimon's opening question: "What sort of God's Son would spend his last hours hosting a dinner party for his twelve best friends who were also his most notable betrayers?"

Ask:

+ How does this question frame our understanding of the Last Supper?
+ What does it reveal about Jesus's character that he chooses a meal over other ways to spend his final hours?

Opening Prayer

Gracious Host, throughout this Lenten journey you have been preparing us for your table, teaching us through riddles and parables what your kingdom looks like. Now we arrive at the meal where all your stories converge—where you become both host and meal, both teacher and truth. Open our hearts to receive not just bread and wine, but your very self, given for us and for the world. **Amen.**

Watch Session Video

Watch the session 6 video segment, "The Last Becomes First," together. Discuss:

+ How does Willimon's interpretation of the Last Supper as "enacted parable" change your understanding?
+ What struck you about his emphasis on Jesus's refusal to be refused?

From Riddles to Reality

Read Willimon's observation: "Along the road and at the table Jesus told so many riddles; he now dramatically becomes the greatest conundrum of all."

Note how the parables prepared us for this moment:

+ The reckless sower now sows his own body and blood.
+ The seeking shepherd now becomes the lamb.
+ The persistent host now offers himself as the meal.

Ask:

+ How do Jesus's parables help us understand what happens at the Last Supper?
+ What does it mean that Jesus moves from telling stories about God to embodying God's love?

The Sword Problem

Address the difficult passage about swords (Luke 22:35-38).

Read Willimon's interpretation: "In asking, 'Any of you have a wallet, bag, or sword?' Jesus is asking, 'When I told you to travel without extra baggage or worldly means of self-protection, did you disobey me?'"

Note the disciples' response: "Sure. Here are two swords that prove our insubordination."

Ask:

+ How do the disciples' swords represent our tendency to hedge our bets with Jesus?
+ What are the modern equivalents of carrying swords while following the Prince of Peace?
+ How does Jesus's later rebuke ("Stop! No more of this!") challenge our assumptions about self-defense?

The Church as Kingdom Banquet

Read Willimon's vision: "Every Sunday is a replay of the supper at Emmaus. Jesus at the table with us once again, as he promised, eating and drinking our way toward the Kingdom. Your church is the way God's kingdom takes up room, establishes a beachhead, a colony of resident aliens amid the failing, failed kingdoms of this world."

Ask:

+ How does your congregation embody Jesus's kingdom banquet?
+ What would it mean to see every church meal as part of God's great feast?
+ How can the church better reflect the radical hospitality Jesus demonstrated?

It Ain't Over Till God Says It's Over

Read Willimon's culminating insight: "We gave our best shot to get God off our backs, to put an end to the constant inviting, pushy intrusion, sly enticing, relentless giving, and the persistent teaching and storytelling. We tried to shut him up, attempted to silence this itinerant parabolist once and for all by killing him and sealing his body in a tomb. But God wouldn't take 'No!' for our final answer."

Share his New Haven story about serving sandwiches during the May Day protests and his realization that this was "the body and the blood of Jesus Christ" and "the kingdom of God."

Ask:

+ How do you see Jesus continuing his ministry of radical hospitality today?
+ Where have you experienced "kingdom breakthrough" in ordinary meals or gatherings?
+ What does it mean that Jesus "refuses to be refused"?

The Ongoing Feast

Read Willimon's promise: "One day, the promised Great Banquet of God shall come in its fullness, and we shall feast with one another and Father, Son, and Holy Spirit—not just for a while on Sunday morning or a Thursday evening, but for all eternity. But you don't need to wait until then to have your hunger assuaged."

Ask:

+ How does knowing about the future banquet change how we approach current church meals?
+ What does it mean that "anytime two or three of us are gathered, and the bread is taken, blessed, broken, and given, Jesus promises, 'Just like in the upper room, I'll be there'"?

Closing Your Session

The Table Setting

Set up a simple table with bread and cup in the center. Ask participants to gather around the table.

Say: "Willimon reminds us that we are here only by invitation, just like the disciples at the Last Supper. Each of us has heard Jesus's call to 'come to the table' in different ways."

Ask each participant to briefly share (one sentence):

+ How did you first receive Jesus's invitation to his table?
+ What invitation from Jesus might you need to accept more fully?

After everyone has shared, read Willimon's final insight: "All I've done is to tell you some of the stories of Jesus so that Jesus is enabled to speak for himself: 'Let's eat.'"

Close by reading the children's hymn he quotes:

> Tell me the stories of Jesus
> I love to hear;
> Things I would ask him to tell me
> If He were here:
> Scenes by the wayside,
> Tales of the sea,
> Stories of Jesus,
> Tell them to me.

Then add Willimon's correction: "On the basis of our experiences of his real presence at table with us, because of the many riddles he told us about a loving God who keeps turning toward us, whenever we break bread and pass the cup in his name, whenever we tell 'the stories of Jesus,' we know Jesus *is* here."

Use Willimon's discussion questions:

+ When do you most feel the living presence of Christ?
+ What is your most vivid memory of a celebration of Maundy Thursday?

Closing Prayer

Jesus, our persistent host and gracious meal, you have brought us through these forty days of riddles and stories to your table. Thank you for refusing to be refused, for continuing to invite us even when we betray, deny, and disappoint you. As we prepare to celebrate your passion and resurrection, help us carry your kingdom feast into the world. Make us bold ambassadors of your radical hospitality, setting tables of welcome wherever you send us. Until that great day when all sit down together at your eternal banquet, keep us faithful at the tables you give us now. **Amen.**

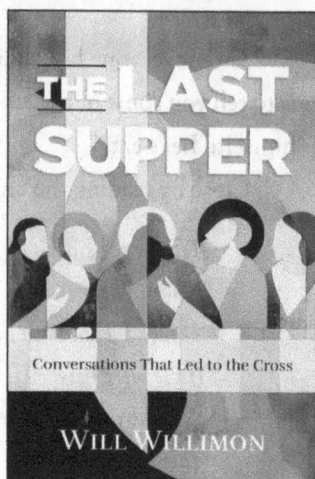

www.ingramcontent.com/pod-product-compliance
Lightning Source LLC
Chambersburg PA
CBHW022111240226
40163CB00007B/20